Moving A Country

Jade Amoli-Jackson was born in northern l
journalism and then worked as a sports reporter on Uganda
Television/Radio, national and local papers. After her husband,
sister and father were killed during a period of internal conflict she
escaped from military captivity and sought refuge in England in July
2001. Her children had been taken from her and are still missing
in Uganda.

Jade's poems tell stories of life growing up in rural Uganda, and
then of the brutal conflict and violence that so many people
experienced. Her writing also provides an extraordinary insight
into the process of seeking asylum in the UK and of making
London her new home.

For more information visit www.jadeamolijackson.weebly.com

Dear Mary,
Thank you for all
your support!
Thank you
Jade
06/06/2014

Moving A Country

Jade Amoli-Jackson

Edited by Lucy Popescu

Published by CreateSpace 2013

Edited by Lucy Popescu

Published with the assistance of the Platforma Arts

And Refugees Network as part of a project funded by

Arts Council England

www.platforma.org.uk

IISBN-13: 978-1489519047

ISBN-10:1489519041

*For the loving memory of Dr. Susan Fields-Flanagan,
mother, wife and a great friend to many and her
loving husband Surgeon Jamie Flanagan, their children,
Dr Sophie, Meg, Ted and their partners and children*

Contents

Contents   vi

Introduction   viii

My Painful Journey   xi

Home

Jade   2

My Grandfather   3

Young Love   6

My Mother   9

My Little Friend   10

Anita   12

My Guest   15

The Man With A Roving Eye   17

My Lone Soldier   19

Flight

Faded Dreams   22

Gone Within A Second   24

Why Do You Come?   25

What Are You Looking For?   26

Visitors   27

Looking For You   28

Myth Of An Owl   30

Moving A Country   31

Run, Run   33

Arrival

Crossing The Border   36

Back To My Past   37

Dirty Me   38

Oakington Detention Centre   39

The Medical Foundation   40

Forgotten Country   42

Britain   44

The Knotted String   45

Walk Of Shame   47

Mirror, What Do You See?   49

My Socks   51

If You Were To Come Back   52

Home

English Ladies   54

Walking For Gold   55

The Present And The Past   56

Live With Pride   57

The Mile Never Ends   58

What A Day   59

Bread And Freedom   60

Journey Here   61

Food Revolution   62

The Marathon   64

Mother   66

Mother Nature   68

Journey To Exeter   70

Acknowledgements   72

Introduction

I joined Write to Life, Freedom from Torture's creative writing programme, as a mentor in 2010 and was immediately struck by the resilience and humour of the group. Working in a safe environment can help refugees turn horrifying experiences and memories into poems, essays, short stories and journalism that shed some light on their suffering and also help them to deal with the problems of exile and asylum.

The cathartic effects of writing are well known. I have worked with Jade Amoli-Jackson for almost three years and am always amazed by the clarity and poignancy of her writing. She is remarkably eloquent when describing the refugee experience and confronting the reasons for her exile. Jade came to the UK as a refugee in 2001. Despite having worked as a journalist in Uganda it took her several years to be able to write in this country.

Some of Jade's work is based on her experiences, some is imagined. Her husband was a captain in the army before he was brutally murdered, but her powerful piece, A Lone Soldier, is not necessarily a direct reference to this. It's a beautifully realised poem about the fallout of war from a female perspective. Some poems, Why Do You Come and What Are You looking for? were inspired by specific paintings at Tate Britain which Jade then related to her personal experiences.

In the title poem, Moving A Country, Jade recalls the abruptness of leaving Uganda, how she ran out of the house without packing anything, 'even my sanity' and her sadness at how the country she once called home had become 'a butcher's den'. In other poems such as My Socks, The Mile Never Ends and Food Revolution she reacts to the problems of adapting to life in the UK with wit and humour.

I've arranged her work into four parts, Home, Flight, Arrival and Home. This is supposed to represent the refugee experience which I think Jade depicts brilliantly, and naturally, through her work.

The first section looks at Jade's life in rural Uganda, from memories of her grandfather, mother and her friends to playful poems about growing up, finding one's feet and discovering young love. She also writes about her school experiences; mixing with different cultures and learning English. The prose piece *Anita*, like so much of her work, is about memories of a happy childhood, but is tinged with sadness.

The pieces in *Flight* reflect the horrors Jade experienced before her escape from Uganda. The nightmare began in 1985 when soldiers from the new government led by General Tito Okello seized her husband from their farm and took him 300 miles away to Kampala. Once she had found out where he was, Jade managed to travel there, only to find that he had been murdered. She had to pay for the return of his beheaded body. Jade poignantly describes this unimaginably painful experience in *Faded Dreams*.

Later, under the present government, the abuses continued. In 2001 Jade's children were abducted. For four months she searched for them, but then she too was kidnapped with several other people, including her friends, some of whom were killed. After enduring two months of captivity, rape and hunger, Jade, aided by a soldier, managed to escape.

Jade's pieces in *Arrival* are about displacement, belonging, and trying to fit in. Once again, Jade's work demonstrates how writing can help a survivor to cope with the difficulties of adapting to an unfamiliar language and an alien cultural landscape. Despite having found safe refuge, the torture she suffered in Uganda is never far from her thoughts as her powerful poem *The Knotted String* demonstrates.

The final section is also called *Home* – this refers to Jade's adopted home, England. Jade has embraced her new life and English culture wholeheartedly but, as her poems reveal, pain and regret linger on.

Most of the refugee stories we read about in the media are negative. But the stories we hear at Write to Life are about the emotional scars of torture and the struggles of building a new life. This wonderful collection of Jade's work directly challenges the negative press given to asylum seekers. Jade's courage shines through her writing and pays testament to the strength of the human spirit.

My thanks to Tom Green at Platforma for originally suggesting that a collection of Jade's work should be published and for facilitating this every step of the way.

Lucy Popescu, May 2013

My Painful Journey

No one leaves her home unless she is running away from some-
thing, or someone has driven her away. I am telling you, I have
first hand experience of that.

We were born in northern Uganda, my twin sister, Jane, and
me. We studied together up to Makerere University, where I
met my husband, the father of my three children. Our father
was a teacher and later became a Reverend of the Church of
Uganda (Anglican Church), in Lira district. Our mother was from
a well off family.

Her grandad had many herds of cattle, other livestock, and
farms. So it was no surprise when her dad became the first
person in her district, Apac, to own a car. Our father made a
good living for himself and became a rich person too. He bought
a bicycle when he first started out, and then a car and a tractor.
We were brought up with plenty to eat and had a very good
education. In class we always came first, or second, although, we
weren't very happy if that happened. When I was eight I fought
my cousin, who was a chief's son: I was number one in my class
in the end of year examination and he was third, but he went
around telling people that I had copied his work. So I fought him
and won. My sister Jane did engineering at university and I studied
media. Afterwards, I worked in television and radio as a sports
reporter and got married. My husband was a captain in the army
and we began our life together.

We had a farm and we had plenty of food, cattle and other
livestock. I had a shop which was doing very well. Part of it was
a bar where people came and drank in the evening or watched
football if their teams were playing. We would really have a good
time, especially during the World Cup when most of us would
support England. I would put a big England banner on the roof
and if you supported another team, you were not invited to
join us. In my country I was considered a wealthy woman, and
my three children were doing well in school. Then, in 1985, the
government changed.

One day, when my husband had just returned from the farm and we were eating lunch, five government soldiers came to our house and said the big man wanted to see my husband. At first I thought they were taking him to a barracks in our town, but when I went and checked I found out that he had been taken to Kampala 300 miles away. I went to Kampala the next day to find out what had happened, but no one could tell me where he was. After two weeks I went back again with the equivalent of £300 to bribe the soldiers who were holding him, only to be told he had been killed. I had to bribe them to release his body to me. He had been beheaded and I buried him without his head. It was the worst time for me and my children, seeing their father without a head; it really affected them.

We went on with our lives as well as we could for a few months, and then my father and my sister Jane were killed by a gunman for ten head of cattle. I blame myself because my sister wanted me to go with her to Kenya and I told her to wait because I was consumed with grief for my late husband. That was the day she was killed. I mourned my sister and my father for a long time.

My children gave me strength but they were not to remain with me. They were abducted on 13th January 2001; to date I have had no news, although the Red Cross is looking for them. For four months I searched everywhere, and then I was also abducted with several other people, some of whom were shot dead. After two months of captivity, hardship, rape, hunger, and burying friends, a soldier aided me and I escaped from my kidnappers. I was a walking skeleton with wounds all over my body, most of which are permanent.

I arrived home, where my little sister and other people gathered when they heard that I had returned, or at least my skeletal body. My little sister gave birth but passed away as soon as the baby was born. Many people did not want me to know about it but I heard their whispers and took an overdose of Valium. They heard about that too and made me vomit it all out.

It is wise to be good to people even if they are not related to you; that's why I am still alive. Before our troubles began my husband and I helped a lot of people, financially and physically, to cross over to Kenya when their lives were in danger. The boy who helped me escape was returning a favour because I had taken his parents to Kenya and paid all their expenses. They were wanted by the government at the time because they were in another political party which did not support the government's policies.

Another man helped me because I had taken his sister's family to Nairobi. Even though I had lost everything I didn't leave my country voluntarily. I had three beautiful children, five nieces, and many orphans, widows and widowers to look after; how could I leave them behind? Even when everything was taken away from me, my children, my home, my livestock and my dignity, I didn't intend to go. I was very ill, unconscious when I was put on the plane. When I woke up I found myself in Britain.

I arrived in London, at Heathrow Airport, on 29 July 2001. I was told where I was after three days; the rest was oblivion. I woke up to see this white man looking at me with kind eyes and the first thing I asked was, where are my children and could he, please, let me see them. I think he said yes but then I went back to sleep. When I woke up again he was with his girlfriend and I was horrified to discover that she was black. Though I am black too, I felt so scared that if I could have, I would have run out of that room like a flash before she could hurt me. I think she guessed what I was thinking and she spoke gently to me. I was in a big bed with a white cover which, I later learnt, was called a duvet. The room was painted with flowers and felt very cosy, but the lights were blinding me so I covered my head and went back to sleep, which I did a lot during those days.

Juliet was very patient with me, kind and really beautiful. After a week I started accepting food, which I did not like at all; even the tea was very different from the tea I used to drink in Africa. She noticed that I did not like the food so one day she cooked sweet potatoes, spinach and green bananas which came from Africa. She also bought tea bags which were from Uganda. I thought, how could she have gone so quickly to Uganda and brought back this food and tea? If you had told me then that I would come to love British food, I would have said no way, but now I like the cuisine, tea and everything.

I started trusting Juliet, letting her near me and allowing her to touch me, and she helped clean my wounds which were all over my body. She and her boyfriend, Andrew, travel a lot to Africa and that's where they had met the two men who helped me. They had become good friends and my saviours brought me to them in London. Juliet told me that she is also from northern Uganda. Her parents were killed and the neighbours had sold their cars to buy air tickets for herself, her sister and brother, and they got out of Uganda before the soldiers found them. She was just 15, her sister 12 and her brother six when they left. Juliet and her siblings helped me a lot with whatever I needed. I was grateful for their presence.

When I was a bit better they told me they would take me to the Home Office in Croydon because it is illegal to live here without reporting to the authorities. They drove me to Lunar House. I had to leave them outside. I was so scared because they were the only people I knew in London, my only family.

Lunar House was crowded and noisy; there were hundreds of people of all colours and ages. Mothers, fathers with children, young girls and boys, older people like me. But why was I the only one with wounds all over my body and why were my children not with me like the others? I cried my heart out, not aloud, but with uncontrollable tears coming out of my eyes. I missed my children, my home, everything.

I waited for a long time and then a lady called me and asked me if I had hay fever because of my tears. It was difficult, as the interview brought back all the nightmares I had been through in Africa. I didn't see Andrew and Juliet again that day or for four days afterwards. I thought it was all my fault, that I was being punished because I am a bad person. That is why everybody I love is taken away from me.

After my interview, I was sent to another section and then another before I was ushered out through the basement into the back of a van. There were two others with me, a lady from Kenya and her five-year-old daughter. Funnily enough, I had stopped crying but the other lady was weeping now and saying she had never been in jail. I told her that since the people taking us were white, there would be no problem. The driver told us that they were taking us to Oakington and that the drive would take about two hours.

My whole body was seriously hurting and I had a splitting headache. I had not eaten anything since morning but I was not at all hungry. I was just in pain. Sitting in the back of a security van was hard enough but with wounds all over my body, it was impossible to get comfortable. My right leg and arm, the entire right side of my body, was stiff. I wanted to kneel but I couldn't bend my right knee. They had said it would take only two hours to get there but it took ages.

On arrival, we were led to a big room. After some time they called me into an office, wrote down my details and took a photo of me. A funny thing happened when they told me to look into the camera. I just opened my mouth wide and put my tongue out as far as it would go. I really didn't know why I did that. Maybe I was losing it!

At around midnight, we were taken to our rooms. We were eight to a room, and each of us was given a bed and bedding, a towel and face towel. Since I had nothing except a blouse, a skirt, a bra, a pair of knickers and a pair of sandals and most of the girls I was sharing the room with had suitcases, good clothes and many shoes, I felt embarrassed. But then I was taken to the office and given a nightdress and a nice lady told me that they would give me more things in the morning.

I could not sleep because I was in terrible pain. I kept turning and crying throughout the night and the lady next to me noticed and told me to tell the ladies working in the office the next day. In the morning most of us had a shower and we went to the dining room which was huge. A man in uniform directed my gently; I was not afraid of him because he was white and would not hurt me. There was plenty of food but I could not eat. I tried to make sure no one noticed but they did, because another person in uniform told me to eat a little and that he would take me to see the doctor.

I did not know that we were in a prison until some months later, after I got out, and read a form with the heading, 'Oakington Detention Centre'. I was shocked because we were really treated very well. We were given phone cards to call our friends and relatives; I gave a room-mate mine because I had no one to call. I didn't even know Andrew and Juliet's phone numbers.

After breakfast I was taken to the interview room and asked if I had a lawyer. I said I didn't, so an English lady called Edel said she would be my lawyer. I told her that I had no money to give her, but she said she was going to represent me for free because I deserved to be represented. Since she was kind, I believed her. She told me not to sign anything unless she was there with me. On the second day, I was interviewed by a lady from the Home Office. I told her, in Edel's presence, my whole story and she felt really very bad and asked if I wanted coffee. Edel was surprised because no one had ever been offered tea or coffee before. Edel told me that the lady was very high up in the Home Office. She shed tears during the interview when I was telling my story and asked Edel to take me to the doctor so that they could examine me and treat me.

The doctor asked me numerous questions which made me cry again because I had to relive my sad story all over again, but she was also very nice. After examining me she gave me tablets for the pain and three sleeping tablets; she told me to leave two of them in the office. I felt suicidal and I think she thought I would take all of them and try to kill myself, and I would have, because I still wanted to end it all. Edel asked her if she could book me in to see a doctor at the Medical Foundation for Victims of Torture. I did not understand what they were talking about because I was not a victim here.

Part of me still felt that I was a bad person who deserved the beatings, multiple rape, starvation and all the terrible things that had happened to me. I thought I was the one who had caused all these people to die or be captured and taken to the bush. If I was a good person my children would not have been seized. My husband, my sisters and my father were killed because of me, so why should they call me a victim of torture? I told Edel not to let the doctor waste her time by offering me an appointment at the Medical Foundation.

They went ahead anyway and booked my first session on the 18th August 2001 at 11am. I think Edel must have intervened regarding my detention because I was told I could go the next day. I did not want to leave because the people working there were really kind and friendly to all of us. I could watch the men playing football and volleyball and children running around, here and there. I stayed in the sitting room lying on the sofa. I felt as though I was the odd one out. My best friend was that sofa. Although there was a TV set, I could not watch it unless other people were in the room. I felt dirty. However many times I bathed I was still dirty, and I could bath as many as ten times a day.

The next day at around 2pm, we were driven by coach to the rail station for the journey back to London. I was given a transparent plastic bag for carrying the things they had given me. I travelled with some men from Oakington to King's Cross and then took a bus to Juliet and Andrew's home. They were very happy to see me back. The following day Juliet took me to her GP where my blood was taken to check for HIV and other diseases. The GP, Dr Cochran, also gave me a lot of tablets for high blood pressure and other ailments. I really wanted to test positive for HIV so that the people who raped me could die of Aids but I didn't want other children who were raped to die so it really tore me apart.

When I went back for the result the nurse told me I had tested negative and that I should be glad. But I was not happy because those rapists were not going to die, they were going to rape other women, children and even men. I felt I had let down all the people who I had been with in the bush. I wanted to avenge my friend and her three-month-old daughter. She had hanged herself and her daughter after they were both raped. We were forced to bury them in a shallow grave. I have nightmares about them to this day.

So I sat near the road and cried when I left the surgery and a man, who told me his name was Billy, came and sat next to me and asked what was wrong. I told him how I had let my friends down because I thought that I would kill the rapists but I tested negative. He was really very patient and told me that I had shamed the rapists and that my other friends in the bush would not die, but if I had tested positive they would have also suffered, even if they had escaped. He said I should pray for my friends who were dead and for those still held captive in the hope that they might also escape like me and live. He walked me home and explained to Juliet what had happened and asked her to keep an eye on me. I still think that if he had not walked by at that moment, I might have done something drastic. I could think of a hundred ways to end it all.

On the 18th August 2001 at 10am I went to the Medical Foundation in Kentish Town. At the reception I told them my name and a kind lady took me to the waiting room which was warm and lively with people waiting for their turn. I had come to see Dr Susan at 11am but had arrived an hour early because I didn't know whether I would find the place. The lady told me to take a seat and offered me a cup of tea and biscuits. At first I would not accept because I had no money but she told me that the tea was not for sale and that everybody was free to have as much as they wanted.

After drinking a cup I felt better. At 11am, another lady called my name and when I answered she said she was Dr. Susan. She was tall, beautiful and very kind. I knew I was in good hands. She told me that her office was on the first floor and asked if I could manage the stairs and I told her I could although it might be difficult. I limped beside her and it took some time before we got to her office. She walked as slowly as me and never complained.

Once in her office she examined me and saw that I was covered in wounds but she didn't make me feel dirty. She asked me about everything that had happened to me and my children, and said she would book me an appointment with the Red Cross. She also arranged for me to see Dr Selza who is a psychiatrist, Mary a therapist and Liz a physiotherapist at the Medical Foundation. I saw Mary in the Medical Foundation's garden full of flowers, trees and fruit. There is a pond which at first reminded me of the swamp which used to be home to me and my fellow captives. But I soon grew to love the space which also had a healing garden on one side. Mary and I planted some plants which were in the nurseries, and I would visit every two weeks.

I joined the garden group. At first I did not like it because I wanted Mary all to myself and thought other people would take her away from me. We quickly became one big family and I forgot my jealousy. Mary really helped me by introducing me to people.

I met Alem who is a support worker at the Refugee Housing Association, and he took me to the Refugee Council Learning and Integration Unit where I met Andrew and Vesna. Andrew taught me how to use a computer and showed me how to apply for a work placement. I got volunteer work at the Refugee Council where I have been ever since.

I did not know that there were people who lobby for the rights of asylum seekers and refugees until I started at the Refugee Council. I have met the most caring people there and I would not swap them for anyone! They are now my family and I love every minute of my time with them. Unfortunately Dr Susan passed away in 2004 and I still miss her a lot. Her husband, Jamie, her three children and Mary are still helping me to come to terms with her death. I have a huge family in the Medical Foundation and at the Refugee Council: Dr Jamie and his children Sophie, Meg and Ted, Sophie my mentor and her parents, and Diana Briscoe. I can't mention them all but I love them and owe them my life! I still go to the Medical Foundation (now called Freedom From Torture) as I am a member of the creative writing group,

'Write to Life' and Lucy is my mentor. I joined other writers on the Arvon course, in Devon, completed other courses and read my work all over the UK. I am very lucky to be alive and attend all these brilliant events.

The Red Cross promised me that they would look for my kids but since the north of Uganda is not a safe place, even for them, it is taking a long time. I hope that one day they might find out what happened to them so that I am able to mourn them properly.

When my letter for Indefinite Leave to Remain came I wanted to tear it up because I was afraid it meant that I would not be able to find my children. But the man who signed for it convinced me that it was OK to get the letter and that if my children were found they would come and join me here in the UK.

Since I had no home or country, I wanted to become a British citizen as the British people had given me love and shelter. So I studied and passed the citizenship test. I applied for British citizenship which was given to me. My ceremony was attended by my wonderful family from the Refugee Council and Jamie's children; Juliet, Sophie and Claire. So my painful journey has a happy ending because I have a country, Britain, a passport and a home.

A longer version of 'My Painful Journey' first appeared in *From There to Here: Sixteen True Tales of Immigration to Britain, Volume 2* published by Penguin Books, 2007

Home

Jade

What a name
It's beautiful
A four letter word
Easy to call and easy to write.

My mum, bless her, told me that I was given that name
'Jade' after my dad found it in a novel he was reading
And thought what a wonderful name for my little girl.
He then took me to church to be baptised.
The Reverend held me in his arms and asked
What's her name going to be?
My Dad proudly said 'Jade'
The Reverend did not pronounce it properly
And said 'Jard'.

Oh no! Replied my mum
She is called J.A.D.E.
The Reverend got it right the second time
My name was written correctly in my certificate
It was unique, I was the only one in my village
Who had the name 'Jade'
That's why I am proud of my name.

My Grandfather

I am laughing already not because I have seen anything funny, but because of my fond memories of my grandad. His name was Luke Ococ Pur Iwor. Pur Iwor was his nickname, which means 'till the land at night'.

My grandad and his children, my father included, would till the land from 5 to 7.30am. Then the children could go home and get ready for school. He was a well respected man. He had plenty of fruit trees, mangoes, oranges and papaw, food in his granaries and many herds of cattle, goats and sheep, and flocks of chickens and big guard dogs who kept his household and animals safe. In those days, people gave you respect according to how many animals you owned, how much food you had and how many women you could attract.

My grandad also had a white man as a great friend whom I think contributed to his fame. His friend was the county parish priest known as the Reverend James Jackson. That's where my dad got his name from, he was named after the Rev. James Jackson. The villagers could see them talking, laughing together and thought that my grandad spoke English like a white man. They would sit on the veranda in the evening taking evening tea, the local brew from my tribe called 'Kongo Lango'. It's fermented and takes about a month to get good result before it can be fried in a big pot, dried and brewed. They would sit on the veranda chatting away throughout the evening and whispering to one another, so the villagers presumed my grandad was fluent in English. They would sit there, the priest well dressed, trousers and shirt neatly ironed (he used an iron box as there was no electricity then), and polished shoes.

By contrast, my grandad would be wearing a loin cloth wrapped around his waist and around his legs, covering his manhood, and some of his backside (most of his bottom was bare). He had a bare chest and wooden sandals on his feet which made a loud noise when he walked. Though the Reverend had given him clothes and shoes to wear, he wore them only on Sundays or at weddings.

On various occasions, my grandad would put on his shoes but would always walk back home after church holding them in his hand or one of his wives would carry them on her head as they did not have bags. The shoes had pinched his big toes, but the reason he gave everyone was that he did not want to ruin their soles.

God only knows what language they spoke, because my grandad knew very few words in English: 'what', 'this', 'come', 'go', and he would speak sentences like 'disdis' (this is), 'yecyec' (yes yes), I go, I come or longer sentences such as 'I there come, yec yec, no no' or 'I there go' The villagers really envied him and respected him so much that they made him the village chief. They thought he was clever to be able to speak to and befriend a white man. Although, he didn't speak English, he made sure his children learnt English whatever the cost. My dad went to school with his other brothers. At that time, girls were generally married off and were never sent to school but my dad took great pride in sending us to school.

My grandad appeared to live up to his nickname, Pur Iwor, as after coming back from the farm, he would take a bath, eat, rest a bit and then would return to the farm and continue working. This is what he led his three wives to believe. But this was not really the case. Word went round that he was courting women and the ones he liked he would bring to his hut, built like a granary with two doors.

This all came out when he married his fourth wife. She quickly became jealous as previously she had been one of the reasons he went to farm at night. In those days, men could marry as many women as they could afford to pay dowries. When he married his fourth wife, she spilled the beans about his nocturnal visits. She shouted at the top of her voice in the quiet of one evening. You have got another woman now that you have brought me home!' My grandmother, the first wife, answered her, 'So it hurts! I am glad you are getting a taste of your own medicine.' My grandmother and the other two wives did not like this fourth wife but my grandmother was respected because she was the first and had grown-up children. When any of his wives complained, my grandad took his spear, a hoe, whistled for the dogs and left without saying a word, and that meant trouble. It meant that he would not sleep with the woman in her hut for two weeks as a punishment. Even when his nocturnal encounters stopped, his nickname stuck.

Young Love

He has been the love of my life
Since we were four years old
His name is James.
We went to school together, same class
We would climb and hide in the mango trees
And talk together as we ate the fruit.

We became close
After we were sent to the naughty corner.
There we were talking and giggling
Like young lovers.
The teacher sprang from nowhere
'Who gave you permission to talk in class?'
Eyes shining with rage like that of a wounded
Lioness, fire coming out of her mouth
'Go and sit in the naughty corner!' she ordered.

We sat so quietly
You could have heard the sound of a pin drop
Onto the floor.
After that, we would walk home together
We brought cassava and sugar in our pockets
For each other
We whispered sweet-nothings
Because we were just four.

We lived near one another as our fathers
Were both teachers at the same school.
My dad was head teacher
And a priest
People thought he was a very holy man.
James' parents were really nice people
His mother was a teacher too.
One day James gave me a peck on my cheek
And I thought it was very romantic
I could not look him in the eyes
Because I was very shy.
Our love flourished until we were eight.
Then the love of my life came to an abrupt end.

My father left teaching to concentrate on church duties
He was transferred many miles away.
I was part of the luggage
Together with my mum, my sister and brother
My dad took us wherever he went
And that was the end of my first love.

Five years later, I was going to a new class.
Surprise, surprise, there he was
With a big grin on his face
Like a cat which has drunk the cream.
'Hello,' he said.
I jumped out of my skin as if confronted by a ghost!
'Nice to see you again,' he went on.
'Hello,' I whispered. I could not find my voice
Which had deserted me.
'What are you doing here?' I asked
'My parents are teachers at this school,' James told me.

We went to a quiet corner when everyone was at lunch.
'I missed you so much!' said James.
'I missed you too,' I told him.
I still remembered the peck on my cheek
It still burned, the spot he had kissed.
He said he had never forgotten me
Because I was his first and last love.
I had also never forgotten him
Though I wanted to convince myself that I had.

We took off from where we had left off
And our love blossomed.
We went to different secondary schools
But wrote every week
Played hide and seek during the holidays
We talked about old times
Climbing mango trees and eating mangoes
Bringing each other cassava and sugar in our pockets.
It was good to be reunited again
Just holding hands when no one was looking
And whispering sweet nothings to one another.

My Mother

Mother, you gave me life
But not life's realities
You cooked for me
But I had no appetite
You gave me a wonderful bed
But I could not sleep
You gave me money
But I could not buy happiness
You gave me love
But I am still waiting for the world to unite!

My Little Friend

Hello! I called to my friend
Sitting on the branch of a mango tree.
His name, which I had given him, is Little George.
However hard I called, Little George refused to budge.
So I thought, as the saying goes,
If a monkey cannot come to you,
You go to the monkey!
I climbed the tree and lo,
I came face to face with a big, green snake
It showed me its fangs as soon as I got near it.
I realised that my little friend had refused to climb down
Because of this unwanted company.

The next thing I did was laughable!
I let go of the mango tree branch
In order to escape this dangerous snake.
(Whichever way I landed, I didn't care,
As long as I escaped with no broken bones.)
As I climbed down
My worst fears came true.
The snake had slithered down before me.
It was as if a tall green belt was stretched
Waiting for me to land on top of it
So that it could wrap itself around me.
I gave a loud yell as I fell.

Next thing I knew
I was in hospital with painful red marks
Down my side and one on my bottom
A broken leg and a head as big as a football.
When I got out of hospital
I limped over to the mango tree
To check if my friend was still there
And was glad to see Little George
Making strange noises, like haaa huu haaa.
He threw me a ripe, mango fruit.
Little George was very happy to see me
Because he didn't have to fear that snake any more.
After some time he jumped down
We went into the house together
In no time at all, my ripe, yellow bananas
Were just a heap of skins on the floor.

Anita

Anita was my best friend. She was born in Pakistan, and left at the age of six when her parents moved and settled in Uganda because they were great Christians and wanted to live in a Christian country. I met Anita at the Tororo Girls' Boarding School, donated by Elvis Presley. We were among the first students there. Anita's family was very rich and my dad was a headmaster and a Reverend who had many cows, goats, poultry, a car, tractor and a bicycle, so I was also counted as a girl from a rich family.

Anita was two years older than me. We did not become friends at first sight, but only when girls started bullying her. The bullies would climb up the bathroom walls to spy on Anita or her friends bathing and so they started to fear having to wash or even going to the cafeteria. One day I saw a girl sneaking up behind Anita so that she could tie her hair to the chair. I stood up and gave the girl a black eye in front of the teacher. The teacher said that I had to be punished, but I explained that I was defending Anita and her friends.

I think they envied her light skin colour, which she inherited from her mother. And as the Pakistani girls' hair was very different from ours, they hated that too. I went to the headmistress's office and reported the abuse Anita and her friends were going through. She called an assembly and warned us all that bullying was not tolerated in school. From that day on no one was bullied any more. I was proud to have done that. Anita and I became inseparable and I gained friends, maybe because they feared I would not spare anybody who was mean. Word was sent to the girls' parents and I became their hero. They brought me food, dresses, shoes and other goodies.

In school everybody wore a uniform as every pupil was considered equal. On Saturdays we wore our best dresses which the teach- ers checked for us. We had white uniforms for church on Sundays. The only thing we had of our own choice was our knickers. I remember I had very big knickers and one day when

Anita saw them she laughed and laughed and said I had put on a pillow case. I saw the funny side of it and laughed. Some girls got wind of it and I was nicknamed 'pillow case'. I got my own back when I called Anita's traditional shalwar kamiz a 'hanging valley', because the trousers looked as if they would sweep the ground when she walked. At first she was cross, but I reminded her about my 'pillow case' knickers and we roared with laughter, kissed and made up.

Anita had brothers and there was one who tried to kiss me. I washed my mouth afterwards as if there was dirt on his lips. I had no clue about kissing or holding a boy's hand. In my tribe, Luo, you could not look in your parents, elders or boys' eyes when you were talking to them as it was considered rude. Whenever I visited Anita at her parents' home, I would be too shy to face him. Anita had a thing for my cousin. They would hold hands when my cousin visited and exchanged love letters.

Years later, I met Anita again in Nairobi. She was married, living in Pakistan, and she told me about her husband and four children. She had come to Kenya to visit her parents who had settled there after Idi Amin chased all the Indians and Pakistanis out of Uganda. Her brother, who was my boyfriend in thoughts and letters, was at university in London. She took me to meet her parents who were really happy to see me. They still remembered when I had stood up to the bullies at Tororo Girls' School. We slept in the same room and talked until almost morning and were very sad to part company as I had to go back to Uganda to my kids and she had to fly back to Pakistan and her family. On my way to Kampala, I thought a lot about my friend Anita and just sat there like a zombie. The only consolation was that we had exchanged addresses and phone numbers so that we could keep in touch with one another.

Anita kept her word and wrote to me and me to her. Some months later she sent me photos of herself and her children. She looked skeletal, really terribly thin. Her husband had been killed and her mother and father abducted when they went to visit her in Pakistan. She was in the refugee camp where they had very little food. She could not work as she had to look after her young children.

'One day,' she wrote, 'God will direct us out of here. I am already fantasising that my children will have a good education and since that horrible man Idi Amin Dada is dead and thrown into hell, we will go back to our beloved country, Uganda, and try our luck with my father's business.' I was gob-smacked when I read that Anita wanted to return with her children and settle in Uganda.

Anita, if you and your children are alive, I am not at that address I gave you. I left Uganda and, sadly, I left my three babies behind. God only knows where they are. One day we will meet again. Please let your brother know that he can have that kiss now and remember my cousin, though married, still goes red at the mention of your name.

My Guest

A knock on the door
I switched on the light
And my guest was there smartly dressed
With his tail as long as
Mr Green Snake's.
I almost collapsed
Because this queer guest is not my cup of tea.

I thought if I ran
My friend will just stay put
I flew out of the door
Surprise, surprise
The guest was as fast
I think it was a competition
Between it and me.

Though my guest was small
It scared the hell out of me.
So the next thing for me to do
Was to jump on my bed.
I then opened my mouth
And the mother of all shouts came out.

My neighbour came running to my rescue
'What's wrong?'
'It's a a a raaat!'
My neighbour looked at me as if to say
Only a rat!
I shamefacedly fled the house
Leaving the neighbour
And my little guest to sort themselves out.

He came out holding the rat
And said, 'There it is!'
The guest was the one who was scared now
And, once dropped,
It ran without looking back.

The Man With A Roving Eye

There was a man in my village who had 'many eyes' as they say.

His ego earned him a spear in his backside. He used to make passes and flirt with any woman wearing a skirt, but one time he went for the wrong woman because her husband was feared throughout the village. Joe would beat the hell out of other men if they even dared to look at his beautiful wife, Lucy, whom he called his soul mate.

Joe had been married to Lucy for over 20 years and they had ten children, three boys and seven beautiful girls. Some of these girls were married while the youngest was six years old and in primary one. Joe and his wife loved one another so much that the elders always gave them as an example of true love.

One day James, the man with many eyes, was talking to Lucy when suddenly Joe appeared from nowhere. He went straight to his hut. When James saw Joe coming out holding a spear, he took off as if he had seen a bull with Satan's horns coming after him! Joe just stood there, aimed the weapon at James and it landed on his bum. James gave a loud cry of agony which drew a crowd.

Other husbands who had been through torture when James had affairs with their wives, daughters or even mothers, were cheering Joe. Even women, who were not amused by this little man's advances, were laughing. As a sign of respect for their husbands and elders, women could not laugh in front of them. So they covered their faces as they laughed, in order not to be seen as disrespectful.

James yelled at the top of his voice and stopped running because of the pain. He could not move, even if he had wanted to, because the spear was lodged firmly in his backside and because of the wrath of the elders and the crowd. The village chief ordered the young men to bring James before him. He mercilessly pulled out the spear from James' behind.

James was ordered to give a big goat to Joe and a big rooster to the elders as penance for wasting their time. For a long time James was the laughing stock of the village. He became known as 'the man with a roving eye'.

My Lone Soldier

You have been my best friend and my love since we met
You were clever in class
And your ambition was to join the army.
Oh darling,
Your hollow eyes pierce my heart like an arrow
Your unkempt beard scratches my soft cheeks.
I think it is a while since
You had a proper bath
So lie still and let me scrub your whole body
Let me wash your long hair.
Barber, please shave off his hair and beard
Which have become a breeding ground for lice.
Your lovely white teeth have
Become yellow, chipped and broken.
Oh dentist, make his teeth white again.

At least for the one month he is home
I will cook nice meals for him
To cover his sunken eyes and scrawny neck.
His ribs are sticking out like tree branches
He has no stomach except wrinkled skin
His bottom is skin and bone
Two stick-like legs and ten skeletal fingers
No meat on his bones.
Where has the flesh gone?
Hunger has eaten all his brawn
So let me cook for him
Good meals for the days he is home.

His cheeks are plump again
I have fed him well
For the three weeks he has been with me.
He has a good haircut and a neatly shaved beard
His smile shows white teeth again
The ribs are in hiding
He is sturdy now.

Today my lone soldier
Is going to the end of another world.
'Bye my love,' he said
'I will be back soon
Look after yourself.'
'And you too,' I said
Tears finding their way out of my eyes.
He turned to go
Army bag on his back
His heavy shoes
And his company
Away in the distance.
Oh my lone soldier
Come back soon.

Flight

Faded Dreams

'The big man wants to see you.'
Everything stopped
Our hearts stopped pumping blood
We could not eat or swallow the food in our mouths
Our children's eyes were wide with suspicion.
In my mind I knew what might happen
I had already been through it.
My friends' husbands
Brothers, even sisters
Were picked the same way.

He put on his shoes
Looked at me and smiled
I knew he did not want
To be shot in front of me and the kids.
At home, I tried to cheer them up
But the dreams were fading away very fast.
I sat down with our children and told them
'Mum is going to find out where Dad is.'
We said our goodbyes, all in tears.

'I have come to take my husband home.'
'We have no idea what you're talking about!'
Then, a young soldier beckoned me towards the gate.
'I know where he is
Wait for me near the market.'
I walked like a zombie to the square
And waited.

'He was killed the same day he was brought here,'
The young man in civilian clothes told me
The man who was in uniform earlier.
'Can you show me where his body is?'
'For a price, the boss wants money.'
'How much do you want?'
'Four hundred!'
I had only three hundred pounds on me.
I was bargaining for my husband's body
Which might already have started to collect maggots.
Finally, he accepted what I had.

He came out still dressed in his suit, headless.
I am at peace now
He seemed to say
Look after the kids and yourself.
I could not touch him
However hard I tried.
The dreams faded away
Leaving only tears and heartache.

Gone Within A Second

Pitter patter
Where are you?
There were six tiny feet, six legs
That all disappeared within a split second
No trace, no words from any of you.

Show me a sign
So that I can come and find you
Pitter patter
Tears I have shed can't bring you back
Tell me where you are
My little ones.

Why Do You Come?

Why do you come near me
When death calls you?
Alone and frightened
I walk the world
I never see you
But the shadows of darkness
Loom near me
Chase me
Strangle me
And I never see you
You're gone forever
Without a trace.

What Are You Looking For?

What are you looking for?
You heartless man
I don't know who you are
And I hope I never do.
Are you looking for
The children, men and women you killed?
The ones you threw overboard
When they were sick and helpless
You refused to feed them
Until they were just bones
Curved ribs with cracks
The signs of torture from you
And your evil friends.

Visitors

My eyes are alert looking out at those coming and going
My mouth opens as if to say something but shuts again quickly
My nostrils open and close
Then my big belly enters
Followed by my bum, thighs and legs
My big toes stand on both sides of the door
They are security guards
My fingers find work
I scratch my back
My thumbs are ready to fight
My neck is strained with the weight of my head
But it doesn't complain.
My heels want to dig in but are poised for flight
My tongue shakes and complains at the strange visitors
My teeth are ready for what may come.

Looking For You

You told me you would be here
Where are you?
I have looked for you
At your gran's place
Climbed where we used to play
In the mango trees
Walked through the gardens
Looked inside cupboards
Behind doors
Scratched my head
Looked behind me
Run around and round
Inside houses
In classrooms
In the church and mosque
Checked hospital beds
Searched the graveyards
On hands and knees
Beating my chest
In search of you
I have searched for you in everything
Far and wide all year round
Looking for you
But you are not here
With sadness in my heart and life
You are not here
No more
Tell me where to look
In my bed, your head on the pillow?
Just tell me if you still
Have breath inside you
Or if you have expired
And are returned to your creator

Just give me a sign
Even if you are not here any more.

Myth Of An Owl

Always, somewhere, the cry of an owl
Sends shivers down my spine.
When I was growing up
I was told that when an owl hoots
Someone has died.
Now I can hear the cries of the bird
Which means that a witch is dancing.
So you can guess what I am going to do.

Run for it
Like a bolt of lightning.
Breathing is not on my mind at this point
I'll think about it
When I'm as far away as possible from the bird
If I get away alive.
I smell death in my nostrils
To make it worse
Night is moving in too fast.
Let's go!

Moving A Country

Move the evergreen trees
Meandering rivers
Lakes and seas
Wild and domestic animals
Birds of all sizes
Pack them all up
In the suitcase of my brain.

Leave behind the soldiers
Covered in old sacks
Or place them on the tip of
My foot
I'll kick them into the deep blue sea
So my head can't remember
And my heart can't bleed
And the dark memories
Can fade slowly away.

I ran out of the house
Without packing anything
Even my sanity
How can a country I called home
Became a butcher's den
And my bed a foreigner's heaven!

I walk through fire
And find no water to cool
My burning heart
Only distant recollections
Fond memories of my youth
And the good old days
I search my head and heart
But the huge dark memories
Planted in my brain remain
I will treasure the good ones
And loathe the bad ones.

Run, Run

Run, run, run
You might never run as fast
As now
Don't look back
At every twist and turn
You'll lose your speed
Run as if your life depends on it.

If a friend asks you to meet them
Be there early
Look and learn
From the shadows.
Don't show yourself
If he is dressed in a suit
Pointed, well-polished shoes.

Look at yourself
There you will see
A hole in your shoes,
Laughing at you
Your shirt is falling off
Your trousers are ragged
Turn and run.

Run, before it's too late
And your friend shows you his back
When he sees your true colours.
Run before you lose all your friends
Yourself, everything
Run, don't look back
The world runs with you.

Arrival

Crossing The Border

The moment I crossed the border into Kenya
I came to the conclusion that I had to leave my past behind
Learn Swahili
My language doesn't matter
No one knows it
I am the one who crossed the border, not the people in Kenya
I will eat their food
The kind of food I never had in Uganda.

Two days later
I get on a bus and return to where I came from
Uganda.
I failed, as the saying goes, to
'Do as the Romans, when in Rome.'
My sister Jane's voice
Rings in my ears.

Much later, I get off a plane at a very big airport
I am greeted by cold air
Slapped right in my face
And I think of the hot sun in Uganda
Which I could not go back to, if I had to stay alive.
My shoes are pinching my toes
I am not used to wearing them
Twelve hours a day.

A thoughtful lady gives me
A heavy jacket to put on
I am warmed by her kindness
But still felt cold
You never get used to things in a day.
The noise of a plane taking off
Made me jump
But I never looked back.

Back To My Past

Back to my past
Children gone in the click of a finger
Husband buried without his head
No life for me at all.

They will haunt you
Until your dying day
You will not be buried
Because you don't deserve
The earth, nor the heavens.

I look for you in the rain water
But find nothing
Hell doesn't want you
Nor does the Earth.

Dirty Me

I try to kiss
Dirty me!
What have I done
To deserve this
Horrible thinking
The sky is open
And the sun shines
To all, but me
When I try to yell
I have no voice.
I am dirty!

Oakington Detention Centre

Dear Edel,

I often think of you as a most wonderful girl, although you might think of yourself as a woman.

I remember you because of what you did for me when I was at Oakington Detention Centre. You represented me so well while I was there. I remember you asking the officials if they had some clothes to give me. I had a skirt, a blouse, a pair of sandals which were worn out, and torn knickers which were my only worldly belongings. They gave me three pairs of knickers, a dress, which I have kept to date as a souvenir from Oakington and to remind me of my troubles from there to here. I also remember you asking the guards to keep an eye on me because I was not eating. They did and I am grateful for that.

You were with me through my ordeals when the Home Office lady was interviewing me. She was, as I remember, reduced to tears when she saw the marks on my back and all over my body due to the beatings I had received from my fellow country men and women. I remember the lady asking you if you would take me to the doctor. You did just that; I was immediately taken to the surgery at Oakington and the doctors treated my wounds, gave me prescriptions and referred me to the Medical Foundation.

I am ashamed because we lost contact and I have never said thank you to you. Kindly forgive me for that and, please remember, although you have received nothing, not even a card, from me, you're always in my thoughts.

Jade

The Medical Foundation

Oh Mother,
You are a mother to millions of us
You are a mother without a colour because your children are all
colours
Black, white, red, yellow and all.
You are always welcoming new children aged between 0 and
100 years
You have adopted us without any complaints
You have welcomed us with open arms.
The first time I came to you I had given up on myself and life as a
whole
Tomorrow was a distant thought and now was not even here.
I think I was just a walking corpse
When I came to you, I could not even enter the building
I was shaking like a leaf, scared that monsters were there.
But one of the girls told me to take a seat, that I would be seen
soon
And then, 'Would you like tea, coffee, biscuits or water?'
Was she talking to me or someone else?
I turned to see who was behind me, but I was alone.
She must be mad
I deserve to be beaten, raped and starved, not fed.
Offering me tea, coffee, water and biscuits will get her in trouble.
I had to think fast.
'I have no money,' I replied,
Ashamed, because I could not afford a cuppa, not even water.
'It is not for sale, I am just offering you refreshment, it's free,
Please don't be afraid, feel at home,' she said.
I was hungry
I had had not eaten since lunch the previous day
No breakfast that morning
I gobbled the biscuits and washed them down with tea.
'Feel free to help yourself. If you need anything come and tell me.'
'Hello,' said another lady, 'are you Jade?'

I answered yes.
'I am Susan, Dr. Susan Fields', she said.
She is white, and not a monster, I thought.
'Come, we'll go to my office.'
I stood up and started limping at her side.
'Oh Jade, I am sorry my office is upstairs, will you manage it?'
I replied that I would.
After a slow limp up the stairs we got to her office
She checked me and booked me in to see
Dr Selza, a psychiatrist
Mary Raphaely, a therapist
And Liz Hart, a physiotherapist.
'I will ask the Red Cross to look for your three abducted children
They will call and interview you in a few weeks.'
She also talked to GP Dr Barbara Wesby about my treatment
(She was to become my best friend)
My body was full of wounds
'Don't you fear my wounds and body?' I asked, but not out loud.
'You're kind but I'm not clean.'
'You don't understand I was raped!'
I shouted very loudly, so that she would understand.
'You're not dirty.'
You're a wonderful, brave person and we're going to help you.'
I started seeing all of them every week
You walk in, you're welcomed
The grass, trees, flowers, even the pond, welcome you
I usually feel great there.
I started leaving my problems in my room
Gradually I started thinking how wonderful life is.

Forgotten Country

What can anyone from the north and north-east of Uganda do
But cry!
The north and north-east are forgotten.
The Queen has visited Uganda
Gordon Brown, the Prime Minister, too
Prince Charles and the Duchess of Cornwall were there
Laughing and smiling for the world
I think they were so pleased by the welcome they were given
They forgot that the north and north-east are part of Uganda.
They were kept in the dark
The Ugandan authorities didn't want them to
See the starving children, women and men
Walking half naked
Barefoot on the footpaths the government calls roads
Children, women and men sleeping and living rough
Because their homes are under water
After the heavy rains which had swept through the north and
north-east
The government did nothing as if the north and north-east didn't
exist.
Since Museveni seized power over twenty-five years ago
I have read, seen and heard about African countries under bad
rulers
And have asked myself, what about Uganda
Where people have suffered untold atrocities?
Well, there are not many white people living in Uganda
Let alone in the north or north-east.
When a white man tours Uganda, he is taken around Kampala
As it is the capital city
Or Entebbe where there is an international airport
Connecting Uganda to the West.
Or Jinja, as it is an industrial town, near the source of the Nile.
Where are the north and north-east?
Forgotten.

Forgotten by the Ugandan government
And betrayed by the world.
Children, women and men from the north and north-east
You don't exist.
They took away your animals, oil, gold and other minerals
And left the north and north-east bare and starving.
The hospitals built by the previous government
Are without medicine and medical equipment
And staff are paid minimal salaries.
Who cares if they go without food and clothing
Or their children have no education.
Children, women and men in the north and north-east mean
nothing
To the Ugandan government.
No white man lives there
To let the world know there is great suffering
No electricity, who cares?
The authorities forgot to clean the roads
They are full of pot holes
Sewage overflowing with faeces.
The roads leading to the north and north-east?
They are still only footpaths, who cares?
Who cares whether children go to school, are clothed or fed?
Even Dr Sentamu has forgotten his people
He cut up his dog collar for the people of Zimbabwe.
In the Bible it says you start preaching from home
Maybe one day he will cut up his collar for the people of Uganda
too.

Britain

You have accepted thousands of different people
To live here with their own traditions.
You encourage us all to respect others' culture and religion
Even colour, because you have accepted all of us.
I have to learn your language so as to know you better.
I can't speak my language
You will not understand me.

I have travelled a long way from my land
Of fighting, killing and poverty.
I want to learn your language so that I can shop
To buy the things I like
To go to the cinema
And understand what is said.
I want to say hello to my neighbours
English, Russian, Polish, Somali and from Pakistan
They do not know my language.

My next door neighbours
Kenyan, Italian, Kosovan
Have started an English course.
I want to learn ESOL
I will study until I get it right
I want to get a job and pay taxes, like everybody else
I want to help other people
But I cannot do that hiding in my room.

The Knotted String

When I look at the string in my fingers
I return to the time I was at the military jail.
I look at it and think, don't take me back there
I want to forget it all and move forwards, not backwards.
It looks at me, as if to say
Put your neck through this knot.
I open one eye and see a small hole
And am glad my thin neck will not fit it
Relief gushes all over my bony frame
I have missed the hangman's knotted rope
Thank you for giving this old woman a chance to fatten her neck.

Then I see a bigger knot.
The man in uniform walks in with his heavy boots
Which sometimes land on my ribs, out of the blue.
I give a painful growl
Swallow the tears stinging my eyes
Smile through the pain
So as not to get more from the boots that are torn
Like a smile.
They sometimes alight on my head, back
Or another part of my body.
Even the eyes get their fair share
I put my face down to avoid the heavy boots
Landing on my poor mouth
Unhinging my teeth from their roots.

He unties the string and makes it into a straight line
I come back to earth and see a different rope.
It's white and thin, without the dark knot I was dreaming of
I am not in that long ago military jail
With the uniformed guard and his boots
I am a free-spirited human being again.
The string is free from knots.
I check my neck and find it has indeed fattened
I open my mouth and words came out
Then I shout: free speech at last!

Walk Of Shame

I was walking on a very busy Oxford Street
With everyone in a rush
For something or other
When suddenly
I fell.
Not in love
But flat on my stomach.
My bag was at my side
As if trying to protect me from the hard concrete
My teeth were intact
My mouth did not hit the pavement.
One shoe was no longer on my poor foot
It had flown back to where I had come from
But the other was still firmly on
Protecting my left foot from shame.
I was wearing my good socks
Thank God, I'd remembered my best pair
(Usually I wear my torn ones
As they are hidden inside my shoes)

If you think people will give you a hand
Think again.
I lay there for ten minutes
Because I could not get up
Or even turn on my side
Shame washed over my face.
'Are you okay?'
I wanted to lie and say I'm just great
Then I thought again
And answered 'no.'
'Let me help you get up,'
The kind man went on.
He had to shift the bulk lying on the pavement
Into a sitting position

And then up to standing.
I was very grateful
But he was not going to leave me alone.
'Are you okay, do you need to go to hospital?'
Checking if I had broken some bones
I was thinking, is he for real?
Why is he touching my feet and chest?
'I am Dr. Matt,' he said.
It was my lucky day!
I assured him that I was alright
And looked at those people who had gathered
But did not want to help
None of them offered to give me a hand.
Shamefacedly, I walked away from the crowd.

Mirror, What Do You See?

I have walked that same path
I have known the pains and joys
Of having a body no one likes.
Mirror, please love me as I love you.

I look at my fingers
Long, slender, perfect nails
I look down at my feet
Alice's legs are better than mine
She has slim legs
Her feet are small and nicely shaped
I check my bum, pull in my tummy.

I stare at my face in the mirror
Oh no!
I have beady eyes
My nose is too big
Nostrils too wide
Look at my head and lo! It's huge
Stick out my tongue
It's not long enough.

I ask the mirror
How do I look?
The mirror answers
Even if I tell you
You will not thank me for my honesty
Just look at Joan's nose
It's bigger than yours
But she thinks it looks great.

My teeth are not as white as Beatrice's
My knees are wobbly
My toes are crooked
Look at my arms, they are too fat
My chest is too wide like a man's
My breasts are sagging.

For God's sake!
Please give your body a break
You're beautiful the way you are
You have a big, rounded African bum
A small nose and nostrils
Your arms are firm like those of athletes
Beautiful, pointed breasts
Who told you your tongue's not long enough?
Only dogs have long tongues
And that's right for them

This is the advice from the mirror.

My Socks

My beautiful socks
Were given to me by a great woman
Mother, wife, friend and grandmother
Dr Susan Fields Flanagan.
I hope she knows that she has two or even three
Wonderful grandchildren.

She visited me in my room and said,
'Put on these as it is freezing
This is winter, you have to keep warm
Or else you will get pneumonia.'
Every winter my socks are there
Ready to warm my feet.

They have seen so many winters
That they have holes in both heels
But they are still warm
Who can blame the socks
They were given to me in 2003
And they are still going strong.

I have other socks
But they are not like this pair
They were given to me as a gift
By a very special lady
I can't throw them away
Even if I wanted to.

Dr. Susan passed away in 2004
I still think of her every day
So these socks are here to stay
I have got others, but they are not
As unique as these
Socks with holes in the heels.

If You Were To Come Back
(inspired by Mario Petrucci)

If you were to come back
I would fly out the door like an ostrich
With outstretched arms
Waiting to grab you
And hug you like tomorrow
Will never come
I will look you in the eyes
Because I will want to take
All those years you were gone
And register them in my heart like
A black book kept in my brain
Sealed with the bond of love

Please don't shed a tear
You're like the sun's rays
That springs happiness in
People's lives
I wept real tears
After you had gone
Life was never the same again
I was dead inside
Come to mummy's arms
She will never let you go again

Home

English Ladies

You English women
Your white skin looks like the snow on Mount Kilimanjaro.
I like your skin so much I buy lightening cream
To make me look like you
But I just turn red and my skin darkens around my eyes.
Your waist is like that of a wasp
Your tummy is flat
I do not think you eat any food at all.
While I go for bread and milk for breakfast
I mean one mug of milk and maybe two slices of toast
And I eat lunch and dinner
A full plate of plantain, or beef, in peanut butter sauce.
Your bum is curved perfectly
God gave you a small, delicate frame.
When I see an English lady
I think God gave me big bones.
I look at your feet, what's your shoe size?
I think two, three or four at most.
When I go to buy shoes, I try to hide my feet
They ask me for my size
I whisper seven, eight or nine, then change my mind
I don't want people to hear and call me 'big foot'.
You walk like you're floating on a cloud
Quick steps, and your shoes make a lovely sound
While I walk like an elephant
Making noise all around me.
Big feet, fat bum, round belly and ears like eagles' wings.
If I look at my waistline, I think
It can accommodate three or four English women's waists.

Walking For Gold

I have walked the earth
Walking for miles during my school days
And always on time
Call it African time.
I had to be in school by 7am
Or else I would be caned
Ten times
Without rubbing to cool the pain
Or five more if I rubbed.
I could have got a
Gold medal if walking
Was one of the Olympic sports.
Right now I will keep on walking
And campaign for it to be included.
Me and my wonderful friends
Tracy, Stephanie, Noah, Hasani,
Aso, Steven, Senait, Haymanot, Achille,
Hana, Serkalem, Tigist, Timothe, Nadine
And all our mentors
Join me for my walk of fame
To 10 Downing Street
And help me campaign
For the walking sport
To be included in the Olympic Games
Ready Steady Go
Here we come, walking!

The Present And The Past

I sat there thinking about the present and the past
Where I am sitting is a far cry from the days of Idi Amin.

When we heard the sound of a vehicle
We would run and hide as we were taught.
Soldiers would come to our village
And find either a meal about to be eaten
Or food cooking on the fire.
Our oven was three big stones
With firewood in between
Lit with dry grass
A pot or saucepan supported by the stones.

Just the sound of a truck
And the whole village was dead quiet.
It came to the point where even the animals
Would just disappear or go into hiding.
As soon as the rascals were gone
Everything would come back to life.
Laughter, a dog barking
Goats and sheep making their usual noise
A mother calling her child.

I turn back to my cooking
Brought back by the sound of an alarm
My food is black
I giggle to myself
And think, I am alive.
It is burnt and turned to charcoal
If Amin's soldiers came back
From the dead
To take my food
They would be disappointed
To get this burnt saucepan
Instead of delicious beans and cassava.

Live With Pride

I am proud of my new country
You walk here
There, everywhere.
Someone smiles at you
You feel great because you belong.
No judgement
No words
A smile is enough to warm your heart.

I am young, fit, strong and alive
Where do I go from here?
Walk the world
Face it head on
Don't ever turn back
Because evil men are after you.

The Mile Never Ends

I walked, jogged and then ran as fast as I could
But my journey was not coming to an end.
Was I dreaming?
The truth is
Whether walking, jogging and running
I am nowhere near the end.
So I hatch a plan
Walking, jogging and running
Is taking me nowhere.
I ride numerous buses
Elephant & Castle, London Bridge, Aldgate.
Then, at last, I get on bus 25
There I see it, Mile End!
I relax and think my journey is over
And indeed the mile has ended
At Mile End you can see it written
And here I am, at the end of the mile.
My joy is short lived, though
For the mile still rushes ahead of me.
And then I realise
The mile never ends.

What A Day

I woke up feeling weak and helpless
I opened one eye which wouldn't stay open
It closed and felt glued shut
The other would not stay open for long either.
I dragged my body out of bed
Had a good yawn and a scratch here and there
Went to the bathroom and woke myself up
With splashes of warm water.
I got ready, filling my tummy with tea
Left the house
The cold air blasted me wide awake
'Good morning,' said a lady, on her way to work
'Good morning,' I answered back.
Is it a good morning when my fingers are freezing
My ears are turning red
The cold wind is blowing directly into my face
My eyes are leaking buckets of water
As if that's the last moisture they have
My nose is sending messages of coldness through
My nostrils and they are competing with my eyes?
What's a good morning?
I peeled the bag from my shoulder and checked for my gloves
Nothing, I had left them at the house
No pockets to hide my freezing hands.
The lady said it's a good morning
All I know is it's a bloody cold morning.

Bread And Freedom

I have eaten brown bread
Made of butter, salt, sugar, water and flour
It's tasty and edible
But I like it not!
Because cassava, boiled and served with spinach
Maize flour served with fried peas
Sweet potatoes served with beef curry
Mingled millet served with chicken in peanut butter
Is the food I like best.

Come breakfast
I have tea with left-over cassava
I did not waste electricity
Warming the cassava
Nor do I waste firewood
Heating my precious cassava
Bread, you call it
Cassava, I call it
Both are food for our bodies.

I ate grass, leaves and roots when I was in captivity
I forgot the taste of bread
I forgot the taste of cassava
So for now, I thank my creator
Who has given me hands and a brain
To make bread
Or turn cassava into bread.

Journey Here

I looked out of the window
Whoa, it's beautiful!
What's beautiful? My friend asked.
Trees, green grass, the people
The earth, I thought.
London is great
But the journey to Cheltenham
Is more beautiful.
Fresh air, fresh-faced people
With wonderful smiles on their faces
Made my day.
The sea of tents
Lovely blue sky
All those tireless volunteers
Children behaving like adults
A toddler trying to walk
But on his bum.
What a day to remember
And I am not going to soon forget
Getting stuck in the loo.
I recalled watching a soap
Family Affairs on Channel 5
And I fell in love with Cheltenham
All over again.
We had the best day
Even getting lost on our way to the station
The driver was also new to the place
All good things come to an end
But it was time well spent.

Food Revolution

After I had eaten a good meal
Fried beef and cassava
Goat curry
And spinach on the side
After this heavy meal
I fell asleep on the sofa.
What was to come scared the hell out of me.
I came face to face with a cow
Wielding a knife and an axe
It was heading towards me with menace in its face.
I started walking backwards
The cow followed me, lolloping
So I took to my heels
Screaming for help
As if my life depended on it.
But the cow was not alone
Was not going to let me off the hook so easily
Because in front of me was a huge rooster
Flapping its wings, as if to say
'It's your turn today!'
You slaughter me, my wife and chicks
And you and your family eat us and grow fat
I mean, huge!
Now it's your turn and you can't hide from any of us.
In front of you are some goats and their families
To your right, the sheep are waiting
To your left are the small animals
All ready to get some justice.
You will not escape by flying
For the birds are waiting with their army.
'Please don't kill or eat me!'
They ignored me and shouted
'It's your turn today.'
They went on chanting, 'It's your turn today.'

With all my strength
I shouted, 'Don't
Kill me!'
I woke up with sweat all over my body
That's strange.
I went to the kitchen and made a cuppa
And the nightmare was forgotten
As I thought of supper which I had to prepare.
The ingredients, well you guessed them right
Chicken stew in butter sauce
And aubergine with rice
Washed down with a glass of red wine.
Let's hope this food will behave.
No more animal protests.

The Marathon

I sat down in my room
And thought about all my friends
And all those men and women
Who walk with the aid of walking sticks
Or use wheelchairs and guide dogs.

I imagined us getting together
To walk a marathon
Call it a race, a run, a walk, a sniff
Or even a wheel
To Oxford Circus.

We would start the marathon at Westminster
And go via Buckingham Palace
Not forgetting to pass the guards
Sitting calmly on their giant horses
Or those standing, immaculately.

I imagine the gentle pat on the back
They get from their trainers
No one passes without taking a photo
Small and large cameras, even mobile phones
They pose so beautifully.

I always wonder, do their horses
Ever get tired or angry?
I am not going to try to find out
I do not want to land in hospital
A smashed foot or five broken ribs.

So we move on with our walking sticks
Some people have two, all colours and sizes
Our friends in wheelchairs and those with guide dogs
All of us have one goal
That is to finish the marathon.

We have a break at McDonald's
I fantasise about the Queen shaking our hands
And come to the conclusion that
After the hand shake
I would not wash my hands for two weeks.

I don't know how I would manage that
As I mostly use my fingers when eating
But bathing can wait
How often does one get
A handshake from the Queen's white gloves?

Hilary, Hubert, Aso, Haymanot
Come for this big event
They bring spare walking sticks,
Wheelchairs and guide dogs
Jane and John join us
Ready to pick us up when we fall.

Mother

Mother
You taught me love
Brought up fifteen children
And all grew up well
And respected their elders
As you told us to do
I love you Mummy.

Here, I have brought
You this beautiful
Long dress
A hand bag
A pair of shoes
But the best thing is
This walking stick.

You are no longer
As fit as you used to be
In your youthful days
So this stick
Will support you when you walk
You can use it to
Get help from a passerby
Raise and wave it
And they will stop to help
The bus will also stop
If you lift it up
At just the right moment.

Do not hesitate to use it
If some man
Tries to take your bag
Use it as a weapon
Hit out fast
He will cry 'Mama!'
And run for fear that
You will use it again
And that the next time
It might get him on the head.

Mother Nature

The sky is blue, sometimes grey
The sun looks down on us with a smile
Bright yellow, then white.
Birds come out in full swing
Flapping their wings
Showing off their flying skills
They could give aeroplanes
A few flying tips.
Bees and butterflies are
Hopping from flower to flower
As their buds have opened up
To the warmth of the sun.

All animals big and small
Can be seen showing off their skills
A cow jumps up and down
As if to say, 'I am big and beautiful,'
Squirrels run in and out of their burrows
Trying to outdo the hare
After a heavy meal
The dog lies there
Under the tree
Dreaming of a big meaty bone.

The tree is standing tall and proud
Its bark is wiggling
Its branches shaking to the tune of music
From the Air
Its leaves are singing and dancing.
Life is good and worth living
I am sitting under the tree
Sipping beer from my glass
It's great to be alive.
Then, rudely, from nowhere
Mr Snake jumps from the tree
Wraps around my neck
Showing me his fangs as if to say
'Don't try anything stupid
You mess with me and I will sink this into you.
I look at the snake with fear in my eyes
My whole body has frozen.
Knowing I could not hurt a fly
It slithers off me and disappears
Into thin air
Leaving me shaken to the core
I think again of Mother Nature
How she copes with all these wild creatures.

Journey To Exeter

Holly, Lucy, please give me a break
I was on my way to Exeter to spend
A whole week with the most
Kind-hearted Annie Horton
When Holly called and asked if I was going
To the Write to Life workshop.
And Lucy, my wonderful mentor, sent me a text
Wondering if I was going to come to our session
That day, 3rd October twenty twelve.

I answered with airs:
'I am on my way to Exeter'
I missed the group and the food which
Comes with it
But I am not going to tell them.
I even wanted to jump off the train and go back
But I had to go Exeter.
The holiday was booked a month before.

It's the most beautiful city
And Annie's home is on the beach
Facing the lake with all its various boats
All sizes and shapes.
People walk along the footpath or are on bikes
Trains make their journey across the country
To London and back, whistling sweet nothings.

Passengers are glued to the windows
Watching the countryside
Move backwards.
Animals of all sizes are grazing
Others are lazing around
Lying on their bellies, chewing grass
Looking at one another
Without a care in the world
No anxiety about where their next feed will come from.
'We're thirty minutes early,' the driver announced
I could see Annie waiting for me inside the station
I got out as soon as the coach comes to a stop.
Annie's home became my home for a week
It was not my first visit.
We went out the following days
Shopping, walking on the beach
Going to the cinema
And we ate all the time.

When I came back to London
I found my house as cold as the inside of a fridge
What a contrast.
I had been in such a warm house
Slept in a warm bed
Enjoyed a very warm welcome.
I came back to earth with a bang
But, love it or hate it, it's home
Sweet home.

Acknowledgements

To my two great mentors Lucy Popescu at 'Write To Life' and Tom Green at Platforma who have worked tirelessly to make the work come to life. I'd like to pay tribute to the late Dr Susan Fields-Flanagan who was my doctor, friend and mother to many of us who knew her. Special thanks to her husband surgeon Jamie Flanagan and his three wonderful children Dr Sophie, Meg and Ted and his wonderful grandchildren. Thanks to Andrew Lawton, Juliet Sheppard and her children, Caroline Goodongo and her family and Michael and his family; Billy Cummins and Edel my solicitor at the detention centre; without their help at Oakington Detention Centre, I wouldn't be alive. Thanks to my little sister Diana Briscoe of Stornoway, who is now in Cambridge for work; James and Susan, my family in Gillingham with their children and grand-children Sophie and Joanna Webber; Hilary and John who are my family in Oxford; my mum and dad Jane and Hubert in Chilham, Canterbury. Thanks to Sheila Hayman, the 'Write to Life' manager, who makes sure that we are fed and our writings are corrected; she's there for us all the way, which has made it possible to bring out the writing in me and all my colleagues in the Write to Life Group. Thanks to all those mentors who give up their time and money to work with us and feed us. Thanks to all my friends at the Refugee Council: Philippa McIntyre and her partner James, Lisa, Judith, Anna, Robert Hartley and partner Rob, Andrew, Warren, Lara Wilks Sloane, Claire Tomkins, Grace Okot, Evelyn Kilara, Joaquina Carlos; Even those who have left the Refugee Council are still my best friends: Almir, Bob Deffee, Jonathan Ellis, Jonathan Cox and family, Joe Leveson and family, Hannah Ward, Vanessa Hill, Gerdy, Chris Badman and his family, Andrew, Ilir, Purmjit, Sandhu, and everybody else whose names are not mentioned; you're all doing the most difficult job. Finally, to all the staff at Freedom From Torture who have been there for me and us all, thank you.

Jade Amoli-Jackson
London 2013

5882304R00056

Printed in Great Britain
by Amazon.co.uk, Ltd.,
Marston Gate.